To all little ones
who make our lives
complete

It's my birthday
and I'm turning five today.
All of my friends are coming
over to celebrate it with me.

This is my friend Charlie.
He is my best friend.

These are twins,
Dave and Eva. They
are my neighbors.

Kyle and Michael
are my friends from
the kindergarten.

I like to spend time
with my friends.
We always have
a lot of fun.

My grandma made a huge birthday cake.

She said:
" It's magical.
If you make a wish
and eat a piece of this cake,
your wish will come true!"

All my friends got mad at
me and left my party.
Even my best friend Charlie.

I got very sad
and started to cry.

My Mom said: "The cake was not just for you, but for all of your friends. You should have shared with them! Sharing is caring. Wishes will come true only if each of your friends has a piece of cake!"

My grandma told me that
she  will make another
magic cake.

My dad advised me to take my bike and to go to my friends.

"If they are your true friends they will forgive you."

I got my bike and went to Charlie's house.

As Charlie was my best friend, he forgave me.

Together we went to see all our friends! They all forgave me and promised to come and enjoy my birthday cake together.

Next morning I helped my grandma to bake a new cake! I wanted to have the best magic cake ever!

When all of my friends came, I gave them the largest pieces of the cake and I left a small one for myself.

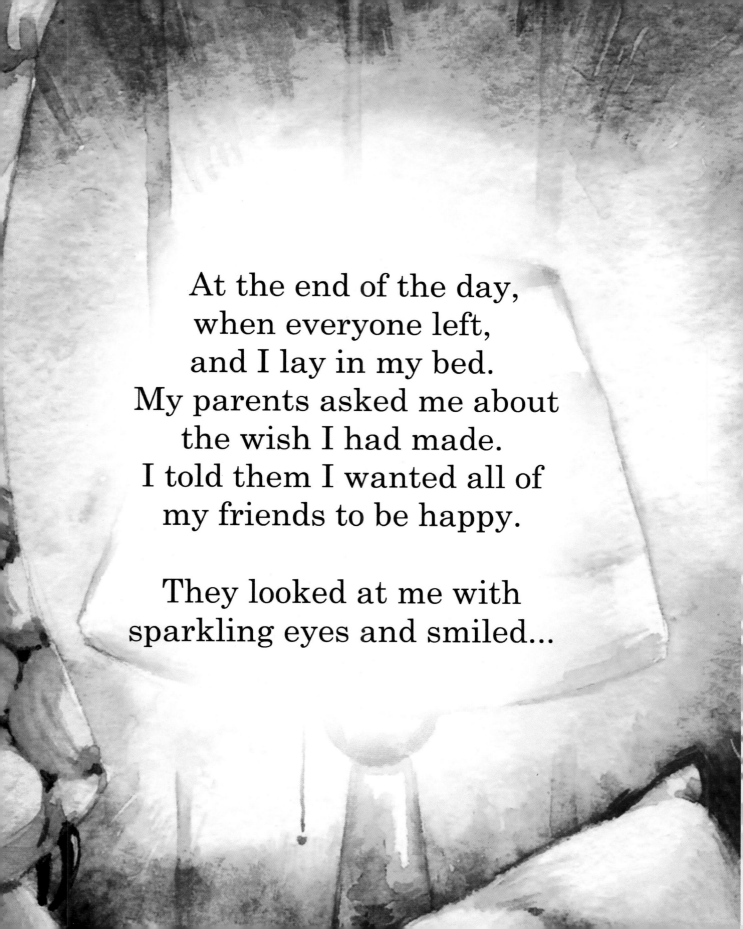

At the end of the day,
when everyone left,
and I lay in my bed.
My parents asked me about
the wish I had made.
I told them I wanted all of
my friends to be happy.

They looked at me with
sparkling eyes and smiled...

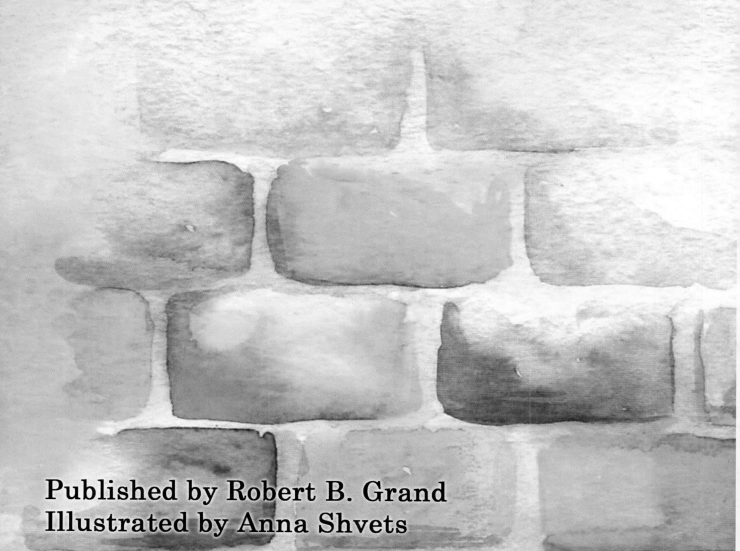

Published by Robert B. Grand
Illustrated by Anna Shvets

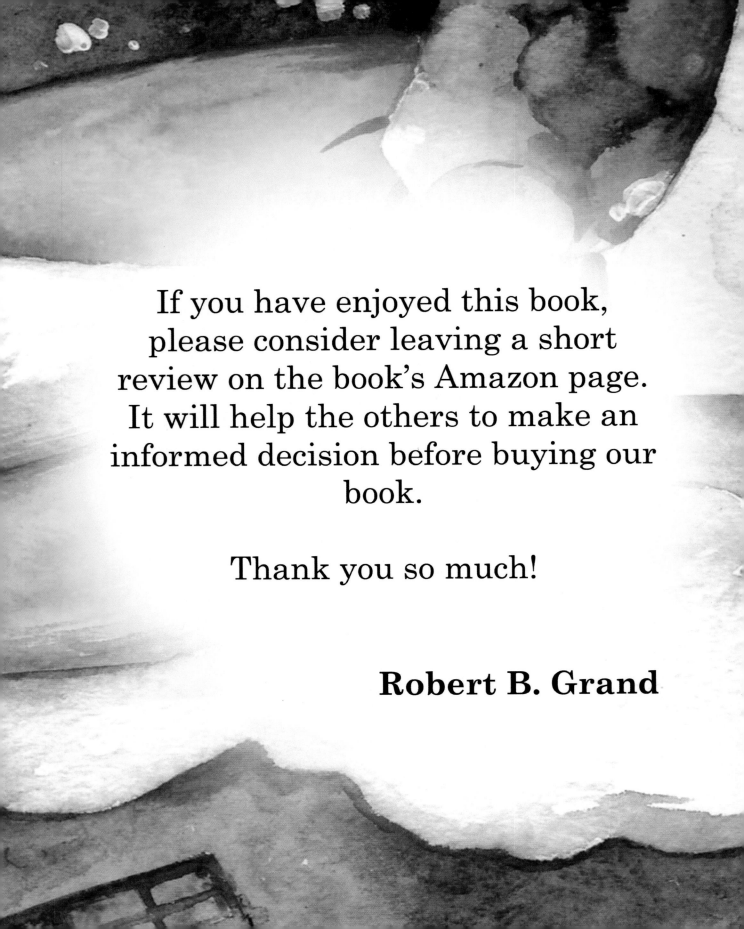

If you have enjoyed this book, please consider leaving a short review on the book's Amazon page. It will help the others to make an informed decision before buying our book.

Thank you so much!

**Robert B. Grand**

Made in the USA
Middletown, DE
28 February 2019